Acknowledgements

I owe so much to so many people, if I listed them all, the producers would start playing that get off the stage music. So, brevity. Thanks to my family for supporting me even when I say things like I want to write for a living and my graduate thesis is about Val Kilmer. Thanks to Nina Sawant, the bestest best friend a girl could ask for, for always being there for me, even from 2,700 miles away. Many thanks to my fellow classmates in the SCAD graduate writing program—for friendship and lexicological sparring and rides from the hospital and homemade lemon poppy seed bread and letting me use their washing machines. And thanks to the faculty of the SCAD graduate writing program, my teachers for the past two years: Dr. James Lough, Dr. Beth Concepción, Lee Griffith, and Jonathan Rabb. Without you, I would know a lot less, and no one would be subjected to this thesis, so . . . you only have yourselves to blame.

And thanks to Val Kilmer, for the movies. They've meant so much.

Table of Contents

The Kilmer Cure

Lynn Schneider

Prologue: Val Kilmer / Me

Current mood: Calm

It is April 12, 2012, and I am sitting in my therapist's office. I don't normally go to therapy; this is part of my mandated aftercare after being released from the hospital. The office is filled with children's games; the walls are covered with kindergarten illustrations, crayon scribbles. There is a book on the bookshelf titled *Hands Are Not for Hitting*. I text a picture to my mother, and she responds back, "No, they are for slapping."

Today in therapy we are making lists, an exercise popular in second grade classrooms. The first list was Behaviors That Aggravate My Bipolar Disorder. I thought we were going to get philosophical, dig deep, but the first item my therapist put on the list was *Not taking my medication*, which set the tone for the exercise.

Now we are working on Things I Can Do to Alleviate My Bipolar Disorder. First on the list—I have figured out how to play this game—is *Taking my medication*. At my therapist's urging, we also add *Talking to friends* and *Playing with the dogs*. She tries to add *Writing*, but I tell her that can go either way, so it remains off the list.

"What about projects?" she asks. "You know, things you do to keep your mind off your symptoms?"

Projects have been, historically, very helpful to me in this regard. Sometimes writing—building stories, building worlds—can distract me, but sometimes it goes the other way, and just becomes a labyrinth of crazy. But there are other projects. Lately, a big one.

"Kilmerfest," I say.

My therapist looks at me a moment, her thin mouth twisting in indecision. She's not much older than I am which is infuriating because she treats me like she's my kindergarten teacher. I'm sure she's a very nice person, but I'm not her goddamn pet. I can see the thought working through her head like it's written in subtitles floating below her face: she's trying to decide if what I'm saying right now is sane.

"What?" she says finally.

"Val Kilmer. I've been watching all his movies. That's my project right now." I wait, but she does not add *Spend time with Val Kilmer* to my list. Clearly, she does not think I am a good role model for myself. "It's helping me," I add. "I get—well, I sometimes get really fixated on one thing, and then I don't really feel better until I do that thing—"

"Those are obsessive thoughts," she says, almost to herself.

"—and right now, that's how I feel about Val Kilmer movies. So I'm really interested in the details and the characters and the writing, and it's like a reward to watch the next one. And the whole time, the whole process, finding the movie and watching it and thinking about it, it's all time I spend not feeling crazy."

The therapist is quiet for long enough that I start thinking about the papers I signed when I started coming here, the ones that informed me that the staff retains the rights to restrain and sedate me should they fear I pose a danger to myself or others. Finally, she sighs, and writes *Val Kilmer* on the good side of my worksheet, which pleases me more than it probably should.

So, Val and I, we don't have much in common. Val Edward Kilmer was born in Los Angeles, California, on the last day of 1959. He was the second of three boys born to an affluent family. I was born over a quarter of a century later, on December 17, 1985, in Nashua, New Hampshire. I was the first of two girls and a boy, and I was born into a social class I once heard described as *po'*—so poor, you can't afford an R. I studied pre-med and psychology at a state school until I realized I needed to add *Working in healthcare* to the bad list, and am now working on my MFA in writing at the Savannah College of Art and Design. Val skipped college, becoming, instead, the youngest student to attend Juilliard's drama program. Since we were both born in December, Val and I have the same birthstone—turquoise—but our birthdays are far enough apart that we have different star signs: I'm a Sagittarius, and Val's a Capricorn. Val is six feet tall; I am, to quote my friend Holly, "pocket-sized." We're both blondes, though my mess of kinky curls approaches afro and Val's golden mane is as sleek as a palomino's. Val lives in New Mexico; I live in Savannah, Georgia. I have two pet dogs; Val has a pet buffalo.

So, no. We don't have very much in common. As far as I know, the man doesn't even know I exist. But we are, nonetheless, inextricably linked. Val Kilmer saved my life.

Chapter One: Me / Normal Life

Current mood: Crazy

"There is no normal life. There's just life."

—Doc Holliday, *Tombstone*

In September 2010, I began burning through Val Kilmer's films. There are some good ones, like *Thunderheart* and *Tombstone*—my life's great disappointment is being too late to marry Doc Holliday—and then there are some truly awful ones, some of which costar rappers. But I have been watching them all, regardless, and writing the kind of reviews that analyze both the screenwriting and the actors' hairstyles.

Val Kilmer is dreamy, and a fine actor, but the reason I have been spending so much time with him is that I needed a project to keep me occupied, because six months ago, I went off my psych meds.

We all want to think we are unique and different. But the truth is, we aren't. It is hardly a novel concept. I've seen *Fight Club* (even though Val is not in that one)—"You are not a beautiful and unique snowflake." We tend to fit neatly into our stereotypes. There is a reason they are stereotypes in the first place; 90 percent of the time, that is how things are. I did not want to be the textbook bipolar patient who starts and stops treatment as often as Lindsey Lohan goes in and out of rehab, but it turns out that is exactly what I am. Textbook. This time it wasn't my fault—I quit my job, and subsequently my health insurance, to attend graduate school. But it was my fault the time before, and it likely will be my fault the next time.

It isn't that I enjoy my mental illness. It's just the devil I know. Sure, bipolar disorder has me emptying my bank account and chasing a bottle of sleeping pills with a bottle of tequila, but I know the rules. I know the pain. Then you go to therapy and they put you on these drugs that make you sick, these drugs that make you itchy and nervous and keep you up for days at a time. It is supposed to be better—it is *treatment*, after all—but it still hurts. Sane people don't understand; they think, well, chemotherapy is painful, but it's still better than cancer. And maybe they are right, and I should just suck it up and work the program, but it's scary. It is a foreign kind of pain, and it is a different set of rules.

Do you know hard it is to win a game when you don't know the rules?

After five months, I was deep in depression. I was not leaving the house; I was making suicide plans. Somehow, due mostly to intervention by my friends, I made an appointment with my university's counseling services. I filled out my paperwork, and I left; they were so worried just over the yes and no answers from my forms that they ran after me, literally ran me down in the parking lot, and had me talk to a counselor even though the earliest open appointment was the next week. They also worked me in early to see the psychiatrist, who promptly put me on a bipolar cocktail. Zombie food. I have been on dozens of similar cocktails; none of them have ever really worked, and they've all made me sick. The last one made me so crazy I had to be tranquilized. I've lost weight, gained weight, been tired, been sleepless, lost the ability to concentrate, itched, gagged, thrown up, worried, cried, lost hair, lost faith, lost hope.

A funny thing happened. A week into my new zombie food, I felt stable. Two weeks in, I felt less depressed. Not happy, but no longer planning my own death, which is a step forward in my estimation. My new therapist, distracting with her shampoo commercial curls and miniskirts, was thrilled; she told me she could tell just by looking at me that I was feeling better.

Great, right? Treatment; normality. I was getting better; I was making strides towards mental health.

And then the problem. My therapist asked me what I wanted from treatment. At first I told her that I mostly wanted to not have to think about my mental illness every second of every day, not to have to constantly be managing it, not to, as she rephrased it, be defined by bipolar disorder. But then I added a toss away, that ideally I would be happy, though I realized that with the drugs that might not be possible, because I'm safer and more suited to life on the drugs, but I'm certainly not *happy*. She asked what I meant by being happy, and I told her I thought that normal people have a baseline of happy. And she told me that wasn't true, and then she described how she goes through a day emotionally.

She might as well have been describing the surface of Jupiter, so alien a concept it was to me. She described feeling happy and sad and frustrated and angry and pleased and content and discontent, all in one day. Dozens of emotions, all in one day. People think that bipolar disorder is constant mood swings, and that is partially true. But your moods only swing between two spectrums: mania and depression. Black and white, when there's a whole world of color.

I do not know how to live in color.

When they introduced sound to motion pictures, many of the great actors of the time were unable to make the transition to the new art form. It wasn't that they were untalented; they were just outdated. They didn't know the medium; they didn't know the rules of the new game.

It's really hard to win a game when you don't know the rules.

I am taking my medication, and I am working the program. I am watching Val Kilmer movies more infrequently, and because he's dreamy and a fine actor, not because I need something to keep my idle mind from becoming the devil's plaything. I am in treatment, and the last time I stopped, it wasn't my fault.

But next time it will be.

Chapter 2:
Normal People / Bipolar Coaster

Current mood: Anxious

Bipolar disorder is in a class of mental illnesses called mood or affective disorders. ("Affect" in psychologist speech refers to the external expression of emotion.) Mood disorders, as you would imagine, are illnesses in which there is an irregular experience of mood. People with mood disorders experience moods differently than normal people. There are three basic ways in which the moods of patients with affective disorders are different from the moods of normal people:

- **The moods themselves are different.** Patients with mood disorders experience a different mood or moods than people without.
- **The duration of the moods is different.** Patients with mood disorders generally experience moods for a longer period of time than people without. The diagnostic criteria for most mood disorders specifies a minimum length of time for feeling a certain mood.
- **The moods are not in response to outside stimuli.** Normal people feel bad when something bad happens; they feel good when something good happens. These rules do not apply to patients with mood disorders; their moods are dependent upon the internal machinations of their minds, not on what goes on around them.

Here's how I explain bipolar disorder to people: For normal people, having emotions is like riding a passenger train. Sometimes you go over hills, sometimes you dip down into valleys, but on the whole you go through a lot of different country. You see mountains, trees, blue skies. And maybe once or twice you'll go really low or high, but (a) these are isolated incidents, and (b) they are in response to the ground upon which the track is laid; the ups and downs come in response to the environment.

For people with bipolar disorder, having emotions is like riding a roller coaster. It's all really high highs and really low lows, and—most importantly—it is not in response to the environment. It just happens to you; you get in the car and strap yourself in, and then you're whipped around all over the place, wherever the car wants to take you. And you can't get off the ride until it's over.

Bipolar patients do not feel emotions in response to the events of their lives. Their emotions ride them, like voodoo gods, at their pleasure. Furthermore—and this is the part most people don't realize—bipolar patients do not experience the vast range of human emotions. We burn at extremes; we have very high highs (called mania) and very low lows (called depression). Normal people may be happy and sad and scared and bored and lonely and anxious and nostalgic and hyper, all in the course of one day. Bipolar patients aren't. We only feel the emotions that belong to the spectrums of mania and depression. Even when our environments do modulate our emotions, they do so along these spectrums. Someone stole my car. Depression emotion. Someone asked me out on a date. Mania emotion. I have a big test coming up. Depression emotion. Et cetera.

Chapter Three: Bruce Wayne / Integration

Current mood: Thoughtful

Michael Keaton, George Clooney, Christian Bale. Time for an embarrassing truth: Val Kilmer has always been my favorite Batman. I was in first grade when *Batman Returns*, the second Batman film came out—old enough to be Catwoman for Halloween, but that's about it. Also, Michael Keaton, not a gift to my aesthetic sensibilities. However. I was 10 when Val's Batman movie, *Batman Forever* came out. More intellectually mature, able to pick up on things like literary devices and B-plots, starting to get interested in boys. And, sorry, Mr. Mom, but Val Kilmer is just way dreamier than you, and apparently even as a child I was this shallow.

Rewatching *Batman Forever* for Kilmerfest was the first time I had seen the film in almost 15 years. By now, I was at the very least the legal age of an adult, and my mind had matured enough that I could dissect the film for literary merit. (I do not suggest doing this with most of the Batman movies It's only heartbreak ahead.) It was on my Kilmerfest rewatch that I realized: Val Kilmer was a horrible Batman. And I don't mean that he's not as growly fierce as Christian Bale, or anything like that; his performance was fine. But the Batman, as written in the script, kind of sucks at his job.

Let's take the circus scene, just by itself. He does not catch the bad guy. He does not take care of the bomb that's about to kill hundreds of Gotham City's elite. He does not stop the three acrobats from falling to their deaths. (He also does not get the girl, but since that isn't part of his job, we'll let it go for the time being.) The problem with being Batman in this movie is that you have to leave room in the script to establish Robin as a serious contender for Gotham Boy Wonder of the Year, but in the process, Batman looks incompetent. So I admit it: Val Kilmer was a terrible Batman.

But he was the best Bruce Wayne.

And I'm not just saying that because I am, as we have already established, so very shallow. He is far and away the smartest Bruce Wayne, the only one who could conceivably run a Fortune 500 company. He is the only Bruce Wayne who is given interests beyond partying and general recklessness. He is the only Bruce Wayne who gets the girl. He even spends a lot of his crime solving as Bruce, instead of Batman.

For a film of this caliber, I was really surprised by the number of images related to being "two-faced" or "effaced" came up. For one, yes, I was a little shocked that Joel Schumacher knew what a motif was, and, as a theme, this dual persona business had all the grace of a piece of space debris hurtling to Earth, but still. We take these victories where we can. The point is, the entire film is devoted to this question of having two identities, of whether you can be two people at once. Harvey Dent and Two Face, Batman and Bruce Wayne. Which is why it's important that Val was the best Bruce Wayne. Usually in these movies, either Batman (in the films starring Keaton and Clooney) or Bruce Wayne (Bale's dark knight) is more like a mask, something separate but not real. In *Batman Forever*, both Batman and Bruce Wayne are fully-realized personas.

The immediate assumption is probably that I'm interested in the Batman/Bruce Wayne dichotomy because of my two moods. Bipolar disorder was originally called manic depression, because it is characterized by two extremes of mood: mania and depression. But I don't view my manic self and my depressed self as two different personas; it's all the same crazy. My interest in *Batman Forever*'s dyad has to do with a separation of an entirely different sort.

I do feel like two people. I have Crazy Me, and I have Walking World Me, the face I put on to live in the normal world. It's something everyone does to some extent; very few people are genuinely, purely themselves in the presence of others. We hold our tongues to keep the peace; we pretend we enjoy things we don't to please people we like. But the level of deception necessary for my day-to-day life is above average. Inside you're in such pain that you just wish you could cut out the part of you that makes you feel this way, but out in the real world—at work, in class, at the grocery store—you have to put on a pleasant face, and be smart and charming. You have to act sane. And it is an act. And it is exhausting.

And it often feels like a mask, like another skin you slip on, another face. But what do you do when everyone knows the mask, and no one knows the real you? How do you reconcile your two personas? How can Batman and Bruce Wayne both exist at the same time? Maybe it's like the uncertainty principle; you can know how fast an atom is traveling, or where it is in space, but not both. Quantum entanglement; you cannot measure one without disturbing the other. They are by nature mutually exclusive. Schrödinger's cat cannot be dead and alive; I cannot be crazy and sane.

Chapter Four: Jack Andrews / Depression

Current mood: Drained

"You get to a place . . . and it just seems like you're just standing on the edge of the Grand Canyon . . . and the wind is blowing really hard. You don't know why you should even fight it, because you know if you just let yourself go and fall off, you won't know hurt anymore."

—Val Kilmer, in an interview with IGN, 2002

In 1989, Val made a movie called *Kill Me Again*. It may be the worst title ever, but surprisingly is not the worst film ever. It's a little noir piece that reteams him with Joanne Whalley (billed in this movie as Joanne Whalley-Kilmer; the two married in 1988) his co-star in 1988's *Willow*, and Jonathan Gries, his costar in 1985's *Real Genius*. Val plays Jack Andrews—runner-up for the year's Most Pedestrian Character Name award—a down-on-his-luck private investigator. He has no clients, no prospects; he's just had his hand broken by hired goons as a deposit on a gambling debt. There's really only one bright spot in Jack's life, only one thing he wants: he lives every day waiting to be buried next to his dead wife.

Depression is the unifying characteristic of all mood disorders. If you have a mood disorder and you don't have bipolar disorder, you have what is called a "unipolar depression," which is just a fancy way of saying *depression all by itself.*

The common perception is that depression is the same as feeling sad, which is, to employ a medical term, a crock of shit. The word comes from the Latin *dēpressus,* to press down. It is more helpful to think of depression as a lowering. In contemporary English, the other common meaning of the word is *to tamp down.* Depression is about sinking. A depression, as a noun, is "a sunken place, an area lower than that of the surrounding surface." Think of depression as this place, this subterranean place below the waking world. This is where you live.

In addition to this "low mood," depression is characterized by the lack of things. Lack of energy, lack of interest, lack of appetite, lack of sleep. Anhedonia, the lack of pleasure. Like Jack, you live in this kind of gray, flavorless, subterranean world. A world where everything you once had has been taken away. I have lain in bed for 20 hours straight, unsleeping, because I lack the energy to get up. And even if I did manage that feat, the world holds nothing for me. Even the things you love most in the world hold no appeal for you.

Depression is stingy; depression mostly takes. There is only one thing that depression gives you.

Chapter Five: Tom Van Allen / Suicidal Ideation

Current mood: Blank

In 2002, Val made a movie called *The Salton Sea*. He plays a man looking for justice after his wife is murdered. This is not a film about vengeance, but it is also not a film about the healing power of love. The movie is about grief, and the fucked-up things we let it do to us.

In the film, Val's character, Tom Van Allen, buys a gun.

The gun is necessary for protection—the Columbians want him dead—and for his mission—he is hunting the man who killed his wife. In Act IV, Tom and his gun come face to face with the man he has been hunting.

Tom is not angry; he has exhausted his anger. All he has left is the knowledge that he must finish what he's started, the calm of righteous action, and the numbness and passivity of an inevitable act. This is not about vengeance. This is a reckoning, this is something that must happen; he is only the vessel.

Morgan, the man who killed his wife, turns the gun on Tom. Tom is not upset; he's calm. He knew he had to get to this moment, the confrontation, but he did not know the specifics. Morgan could die, or he himself could. Tom even says it (twice!), "It doesn't matter."

As long as Morgan dies, or Tom does, the act, this inevitable act, is complete. It is only when Morgan pulls the trigger and finds Tom's gun empty that Tom springs into action, injecting Morgan with an abandoned syringe. And then, another surprise. Tom picks up Morgan's gun, and he puts it to his own head. Before Morgan is dead.

This act is not about revenge; it's about absolution. It is about inevitable conclusion; Tom should have died in that house at the Salton Sea; he should have died with his wife. Blood must be paid for his wife's, but it doesn't matter whose; they are both equally culpable.

And so Tom Van Allen holds a gun to his head. The barrel is still warm from previous rounds fired into bad men, the sear kissing his temple. It is not his gun; the gun belongs to a dying man, the man who killed his wife at the Salton Sea, the man who should have killed Tom that same night. Fate is funny like that. Tom watches the dying man struggling for breath, and he holds the gun to his own head.

For the bipolar patient, suicide is one of life's constants. Suicide is a roommate with an on-again, off-again steady beau; sometimes you don't see them for weeks, and then, all of a sudden, they're everywhere, all up in your face, leaving their shit everywhere, and marathoning *The Hills* while you're trying to sleep.

The medical term is "suicidal ideation." It means literally that your brain, abnormally, entertains the idea of self-termination. What this cold, clinical term does not explain is that it isn't a choice.

Suicidal ideation does not mean that your crazy brain simply comes with the after-market upgrade that gives you the option to entertain these ideas. It means that, occasionally, your brain is taken over by these ideas; these thoughts come like compulsion, unbidden and too quick to dodge.

You walk across a bridge on your way to Starbucks, the same way you walk every day, and you're thinking of a macchiato until your brain is taken over and all channels are you climbing up on the railing, letting your body go to gravity.

You do not engineer these thoughts; they possess you.

In a strip of Bill Watterson's *Calvin and Hobbes*, the young boy Calvin sits on a sled atop a snowy hill. Below him, the road is fraught with obstacles, and Calvin considers them one by one. At the end, he declares, "My brain is trying to kill me." This is life for the depressed patient with suicidal ideation. Your brain is trying to kill you.

The walls of my bedroom are yellow. It's kind of like how hospitals paint recovery rooms pale blues and greens—soothing colors. You are not feeling soothed, so they try to trick you with a couple gallons of semi-gloss. It's the same idea: I am not cheerful, but maybe I can be tricked into being cheerful.

It doesn't work. I am 14, and it is my first time. The scene has played itself out in my head a thousand times, until the details are gem-brilliant. I have not practiced, but my body knows what to do; it feels like I was made for this.

My first time, I take a bottle of Tylenol PM, one enteric-coated pill after another sliding smoothly down my throat. Tylenol is a word-association-game kind of choice: Tylenol kills pain; what I want gone isn't me but the pain that lives inside me. You take medicine when you feel bad; there does not seem to be any kind of medicine made to help with this, so I take what I have.

It is strangely comforting, the rote action of swallowing one pill after another, a hundred, a whole bottle. The comfort that you are finally doing something to combat this thing that is killing you. That you will kill it, even if it kills you in the process.

There is a bright side to suicide, a comfort. Most people who have never lived with these thoughts, who have never considered these actions, imagine that it's all heartache, that suicide is all wretched emotions, all crying and calling out to God, the way they themselves would face death. And there is a lot of that; if we felt well, we would not want to kill ourselves. But there is also a great calm, a strange sliver of joy; you have an escape plan. You feel like you have just discovered a super power, or made a scientific breakthrough: there is a way out. You've found a way out.

But how does suicidal ideation become the suicide attempt? The tipping point is wildly misunderstood by people whose brains do not work this way. The common perception is, you cross the line at the lowest depths of your misery. You kill yourself because you have never been sadder.

Wrong again, sane people. The human mind is a crucible; we have capacity for endless depths of emotions. The tipping point comes the same way every time. You reach a point where you believe—absolutely, with religious conviction—not that there is no bottom to your sadness, but that there is no end to it. You will feel like this forever.

Obviously, something has to be done.

My belly is full of Tylenol PM. Unsurprisingly, I sleep.

Tom Van Allen, eyes sparked with tears, lowers the gun. He aims squarely at the dying man's weak flesh, and empties the chamber, laughing.

Here are things I don't know. I don't know how to divine Planck's constant. I don't know why Kim Kardashian is famous. I don't know why I didn't die that night after taking a whole bottle of Tylenol. I don't know whether there are permanent effects. What I do know is that it is notoriously difficult to kill yourself. I know that there are a whole lot of things I am not good at, and maybe suicide is just another one of those. Whatever the cause, I wake up the next morning as if it is just another morning, as if nothing has happened. My family affects their usual willful blindness, and if they noticed anything amiss, they say nothing.

The thing about living with bipolar disorder is that it teaches you to roll with the punches. If you got your panties in a twist every time you tried to kill yourself, you'd never get anything done. You crest the peak of raw emotions and emerge on the other side, whole. It's a new day.

Chapter Six: Montgomery / Mania

Current mood: Chipper

Bipolar disorder is characterized by extremes of mood: low lows (depression) and high highs (mania). There are two forms of bipolar disorder: bipolar I and bipolar II. These subsets are differentiated from unipolar depression, and one another, by mania. Bipolar I patients suffer from full manic episodes, periods of mania lasting several days to a month. I have bipolar II; bipolar II patients suffer from hypomania, from the Greek *hypo*, meaning *under*, a less severe form of mania. Full mania is characterized by hallucinations and general life-ruining; hypomania is the romantic mania of film and television, wherein you become creative and charming and euphoric.

Not that hypomania cannot be equally as life-ruining, or terrifying. To use the roller coaster analogy again: when you're manic you're high, you're going a thousand miles an hour—and you're strapped in, completely out of control. When I'm manic, even if I'm having a great time, I'm not driving. Something else is in control. It's exhilarating, terrifying.

Here's the math people do to divine *mania*:

depression = super sad

mania = the opposite of depression

mania = super happy

Well, sure, sometimes. But why would we need mania medicated away if all it was nothing but happiness?

The last time I was manic, I had to be tranquilized.

Just as depression is less sadness than it is "low mood" (as we have discussed), mania is more properly "high mood." Anxiety, euphoria, anger, agitation—mania is less a specific emotion in itself than it is other emotions amplified.

Where depression is a subtraction, characterized by a lack of things, mania is *more* of everything. I had to be tranquilized because I could not calm down; my anxiety level was so high it was like a days-long panic attack. Mania is full volume, full throttle. Too much energy for sleep, too much luck to lose, too much hubris for surrender. Manic patients get in trouble gambling and spree shopping and driving 120 miles an hour. You are too full to be contained; there are no consequences, and—even when you begin to come down, and you can see downsides—there are no brakes.

Truth time: I bought *The Island of Dr. Moreau* off Amazon for a dollar and shipping because I wanted to watch Val Kilmer imitate Marlon Brando. The film is based on a novel by H.G. Wells; I haven't read the book, but I have seen other adaptations of it. Mostly in cartoons; they did it on *The Simpsons*, and I think on the *Batman* animated series. The movie actually came out on the book's centennial; it was originally published in 1896.

Val's character, Montgomery, spends most of the movie manic, though his erratic behavior is less from mental illness and more from the fact that his blood is composed of about 75 percent home-brewed heroin.

Montgomery's increasingly erratic behavior ruins his career, and eventually leads to his death. And yet the whole time he never hesitates; mania is a *damn the torpedoes, full speed ahead!* good time.

Chapter Seven: Doc Holliday / Self-Destruction

Current mood: Exanimate

"Nonsense. I have not yet begun to defile myself."

—Doc Holliday, *Tombstone*

Bipolar disorder is a study in excess. By definition, these excesses are of mood: the highest highs and the lowest lows. In practice, excess is everywhere.

Especially in bad neighborhoods.

There is a high comorbidity—that is a medical word loosely translated to, "you got screwed twice by the same dealer"—between bipolar disorder and substance abuse. Given how prone bipolar patients are to bucking their officially sanctioned psych meds, it's sometimes difficult to understand why so many of us are so eager to self-medicate. And yet . . .

Alcohol is legal, which for some reason is translated in the common vernacular as "harmless." This is far from the case, especially in college. When people wanted to go out drinking—which was all the time—I had to be careful in accepting. Some nights, it was fine: it was possible to have one drink and apply the brakes. No problemo. And some nights, one drink became ten more, and after the friends you came with went home there were more friends: Misters Beam and Daniels. Nice, Southern gentlemen. Always willing to help a girl in need.

The temptation to numb, to drink and smoke the negative feelings away, is always great. Even if you're on meds, the temptation to self-medicate is there. The key is self regulation.

Substance abuse is a slow form of self-destruction. The most keen self-destruction is called self-injury, or SI. SI is just what it sounds like: purposeful injury of the self. The methods of SI are varied, though cutting is the best known. I prefer blunt trauma because it leaves bruises, not scars, although the first time I SI'd I burned myself with a hot glue gun, which left a scar that is still there, 12 years later.

SI may be more difficult to understand than suicidal ideation. Why would anyone purposefully hurt themselves? Avoiding pain is more or less our entire aim as human beings, right?

In 1993, Val stole a little western called *Tombstone* right out from under Kurt Russell's ridiculously mustachioed nose. Val plays dentist-turned-gunslinger Doc Holliday, deep into his *dying of tuberculosis* thing. Doc is a very smart man; he's a doctor and classically educated. He speaks Latin. He quotes Shakespeare. He understands the consequences of his actions.

It's just that his better sense gets overridden. He cannot help himself. Doc tends—gleefully—toward chaos. Self-destruction isn't just a byproduct of his lifestyle; it's a good time!

Doc, who should be in bed resting after collapsing from a consumptive attack the day before, joins the Earps for the shootout at the OK Corral. The Earps are tense, faces drawn. Doc whistles, and tips his hat to the women he passes. As they make the Corral, Virgil gives the order to the cowboys to disarm; they are breaking the law carrying guns in town. Both sides draw their weapons; everyone goes still, breathless in anticipation of the next act. It's a standoff.

Billy Clanton is shaking, sweating. Doc catches his eye.

And winks.

Doc tends—barrels—toward chaos. For him, the waiting is a thousand times worse than anything that could happen once the shooting starts. And so he cannot help himself from being the straw that breaks the camel's back. Chaos reigns.

Self-destruction is inherent to many mental illnesses. There's a theory floating around that the instinct for self-preservation is the foremost tenet of sanity. I could quote Freud.

Crash course: Freud believed the human subconscious was broken into three parts: the ego, the superego, and the id.

The ego is "I"; it is the basic working unit of your waking mind.

The superego is the imposition on the ego of all societal influence—everything your parents or your preacher ever told you about right and wrong lives in the superego.

The id is the ego's antagonist, the seat of all primal urges. When your mother tells you that you can't have any more candy, it'll rot your teeth, the id wants. That. Candy. When the police tell you that you have to stop for red lights, not to do so is a crime, the id has your foot itching to press down on the accelerator.

The id's desires are broken into two conflicting forces: Eros, the life force; and Thanatos[1], the death force. The life force is what wants all those things that tend toward life (meaning, as you may suspect if you are even casually familiar with that horny old goat, Sigmund, *sex*). Eros is the desire for sex, for propagation, for babies. Thanatos, the death drive, is the opposite. Thanatos craves destruction. In normal psyches, Thanatos is simply a counterbalance to Eros, and centers mostly on the human realization that all things, including themselves, will one day die. In abnormal psyches, like those of people who have undergone trauma or are plagued by mental illness, Thanatos takes on a life of its own.

Expressions of the death drive can take two forms: external or internal. External expressions of Thanatos involve harming others, or destroying things

[1] Thanatos, like Eros, was a god in Greek and Roman mythology. Thanatos was the iron-hearted god of death, and generally a guy that no one wanted to party with.

outside of one's self: murder, fire setting, etc. Internally-focused expressions of Thanatos involve things like suicide.

Suicide is the most dramatic form of self-destruction. Suicide rates are highest among patients with mood disorders; suicide rates among patients with bipolar disorder fall somewhere between 15 and 20 percent, or some 30 times higher than the national average.

Self-destruction is also evident in behaviors like habitual drug and alcohol use, and binging and purging behaviors in patients with eating disorders. Even with its staggering suicide rates, bipolar disorder is second in overall mortality rates among mental illnesses, falling behind eating disorders, which have an overall death rate of about 20 percent even though the suicide rates are lower. Though the aim of anorexia is not to end one's life, death is often the outcome.

The most popular form of SI is cutting, although there are many other alternatives, from beating and burning to trichotillomania, in which patients compulsively pull out their own hair[2]. What does the typical self-injurer look like? She is a woman in her 20s or 30s. She has been self-injuring since she was a teenager, and she most likely has a history of physical or sexual abuse and/or suffers from an eating disorder, a mood disorder, or borderline personality disorder. She is smart and well-educated. She probably discovered SI spontaneously, and has a favorite method, though the Internet has, like the pro-ana movement[3], created a community in which she can learn to be a better self-injurer. She is probably very good at hiding it.

I am the typical self-injurer. I am 26, and have been self-injuring since the eighth grade. I have bipolar disorder. I am in graduate school. I discovered SI on my

[2] Do not confuse trichotillomania with the use of depilatory products, in which unwanted hair is removed via waxing, plucking, or threading. Patients suffering from trichotillomania pull out their hair until they have large bald patches; sometimes the hair is then chewed and/or ingested.

[3] "Pro-ana" stands for "pro-anorexia." The Internet has created something of a support group for eating disorder sufferers, glamorizing the impossibly slender physiques of their "thinspirations" (thin + inspiration), and teaching tips on how to be a better—that is, thinner and less healthy—anorexic.

own, like you discover sex: like it's something new and magical you can't believe no one had thought of before.

I am excellent at hiding it.

Razor blades come in packs of 10 or 100. You always buy the 10-pack, because there's no way you'll need 100, you think. You're not going to be doing this that long.

There's something in your chest, in your blood, that wants out, something you can feel itching for release. The tension is unbearable, or else you wouldn't be doing this. It's not like you're some kind of freak.

Razor blades are beautiful, in their way; there's a starkness to them, a simplicity of line and shape and function that is pleasing. You pick one from your box of 10, feel the weight of it in your hand. Maybe test the edge with your fingertip; a single drop of blood, the color and luminosity of a Burmese ruby, beads up, smears rust-colored across the steel.

You draw the razor blade across your skin, watching your flesh open up, watching all your pain and anxiety and frustration bleed out.

Though some people mix and match their methods of SI, most self-injurers, like bomb makers, find their special formula and stay with it. The three big ones are cutting, beating, and burning.

Cutting is by far the most common form of self-injury. When cutters cut, they use a razor, knife, or other sharp object to deliberately break the skin. Cutting can be done anywhere on the body but is usually done on the forearm opposite the dominant hand or on the thighs, places which are easy to reach without contorting oneself into exotic positions.

For many years, bloodletting was a popular medical procedure, used to treat everything from scurvy to syphilis[4]. Bloodletting has its roots in medieval times, when all ills were blamed on an imbalance of humors. For those of you who did not

[4] Other medieval syphilis cures include: arsenic, taken orally, and mercury, applied to the, er, trouble areas.

attend medieval medical school, humors were substances that fought for balance in your body. The four humors were blood, phlegm, black bile, and yellow bile. Each humor corresponded with a different set of personality traits, and an imbalance of humors was thought to be the cause of disease, and was easily diagnosed by studying the personality trait affected and its corresponding humor. For example, if you suffered from irritability, you had too much bile. If you were catatonic, you had too much phlegm. Et cetera. Bloodletting (along with modifications of diet and exercise to affect the balances of one's phlegm and biles) was simply an attempt to realign the humors[5].

In cutting, blood is half the point. Bleeding is so important to the process of cutting that, in treatment, cutters are urged, instead of cutting themselves, to draw red lines on themselves with marker. Many self-injurers report pleasure in seeing a physical change in their bodies, a change they caused, be it blood or bruises or burns.

Blunt trauma is another form of self-injury. The most common type of blunt trauma SI is wrist banging, in which the self-injurer repeatedly hits the head of the ulna (the large bone on the outside of the wrist) on a solid object. This can cause bruising and broken bones. There is also head banging, in which self-injurers hit their head into a wall or other solid surface. Other forms of blunt trauma include injurers hitting themselves with their fists or objects like wire hangers.

Self-flagellation is a religious act that has been practiced since the 13th century. Monks would beat themselves with whips and knotted cords, often while chanting about what a good guy this God who invented whips and knotted cords was. Originally started as homage to events during Christ's Passion, self-flagellation evolved into a movement in which penitents revered suffering as the only way to guarantee a clean soul and passage to heaven.

---

[5] Bloodletting is still a viable therapy for some conditions, like hemochromatosis ("bronze diabetes," a condition in which there is too much iron present in the blood.)

Ironically, a study by Russian scientists in 2005 suggests that being whipped curbs depression, suicidal thoughts and actions, and addiction[6]. The Russian scientists cite corresponding release of endorphins as the culprit. Endorphins are neurotransmitters (chemical messengers that work in the brain) that produce a feeling of well-being. Part of the peripheral nervous system, which governs the flight or fight response, endorphins are released during pain and excitement but also during sex and love[7]. Part of the pleasurable sensation you feel while spending time with your loved one or after orgasm is from endorphins.

Burning is another popular form of self-injury. Burning is done in a variety of different ways: with matches, an open flame, a hot object, chemicals, etc. The first time I self-injured, I burned myself with a hot glue gun, letting the molten glue stick to my skin until it had hardened and cooled enough to be removed. Matches are a popular tool for burning; the matches are lit, and held to the skin to extinguish. This method is relatively safe in the world of burning; there's less chance of anything catching fire from ambient flame.

Branding is the act of purposefully leaving a permanent mark on the flesh via application of an extremely hot object. Human branding was practiced during the years of slavery; contemporarily it is used by some tribes as a rite of passage. Human branding has also found popularity in BDSM[8] communities. Here, both the brand itself and the act of branding are found pleasurable.

---

[6] The study was carried out by Dr. Sergei Speransky, et al., at the Novosibirsk Institute of Medicine, 2005.

[7] And while eating chocolate.

[8] BDSM stands for "bondage, discipline, sadomasochism," and is a group of sexual behaviors in which pain and submission are found erotic. For more information about BDSM, I generally do not advise Googling "BDSM." There is some crossover between self-injurers and BDSM activities; it's simply switching from causing pain to yourself to having someone else cause it. J, a friend who was willing to talk to me about her own self-injury, says, "Getting on antidepressants and getting some good therapy (primarily Cognitive Behavioral Therapy) helped a lot [in stopping SI], and getting involved in BDSM pretty much extinguished the behavior."

For people who have never had the urge to do it, self-injury seems, well, crazy. Most people have a death drive that merely serves to balance out their life force; most people are too interested in self-preservation to entertain the idea of hurting themselves on purpose. Yet thousands of people, many of them children, regularly practice these behaviors. There must be a reason why, right?

There are multiple reasons. The first has to do with control. Self-injurers feel out of control in their environment; they feel out of control in the wake of the mental illness that lives inside them[9]. Self-injurers cannot control the pain they feel on the inside, so they control the pain they feel on the *outside* by deliberately causing it.

It's also a distraction from your problems. SI becomes a ritual, and rituals are soothing, especially when they can put blinders on you to the stressors in your life. SI becomes a little project, something you do so you're not spending time with your depression or your anxiety or your abusive household. T, a friend who was willing to talk to me about her own self-injury, says, "Whenever I did it, it made me feel almost like I'd accomplished something, for a little while. I'd be concentrating really hard on the SI, and then it'd be done and I could wrap it up. That feeling wouldn't last long, though; usually when the bandage fell off and I saw the SI site again, I'd start having the itch to do it again. It was definitely about reestablishing a sense of control."

And we cannot forget the endorphins, the stars of the Russian whipping study. Here's the math: pain causes endorphins. Endorphins make you feel better, if only for a moment. Pain makes you feel better.

Self-injury is a coping strategy, but it's not a healthy coping strategy. How do self-injurers stop self-injuring?

Some self-injurers stop on their own. They either leave the situation that was causing them such stress in the first place, or they simply grow out of the behavior.

---

[9] Anorexia, especially, is characterized by its desire for control, for perfection; there is a very high comorbidity between anorexia and self-harm behaviors.

T says, "When I stopped SIing, it wasn't for any particular reason. Possibly I had a little more room in my life to just be depressed instead of anxious and depressed at the same time."

Others need help to stop. There are therapies to counteract the urge to self-injure. Antidepressants are by far the most helpful, though some cases may require ongoing psychotherapy, in which patients are taught aversion therapies and healthy ways to manage their negative feelings. There are even specialized in-patient rehabilitation programs. Unfortunately, there are very few studies on SI as a whole[10] and less information still about things like recidivism rates, so there's no real way to make sure these things are effective long-term options. And stopping the behavior doesn't mean that the scars—both literal and figurative—from the disease are gone. L says, "It's been eight years since the last [time I self-injured]. Thinking back, I mostly just miss it." It's like AA; no matter how many days of clean living you have behind you, you always miss it. The urge is always there.

But, as we've discussed, there are a lot of "slow" forms of self-destruction; there are a lot of human behaviors that negatively affect our health and our lives. T says, "The period in which I SI'd overlapped to a certain extent with the period in which I started doing other things that are detrimental to my health, and I am still doing them every day." People drink too much, smoke too much, eat too much. They do drugs; they drive too fast. What makes those behaviors personality traits, and SI pathological? It isn't just the passage of time; self-injury has a historical basis. It has been going on for centuries, long before there were cars to drive too fast. What makes one a quirk, and one a disease? Is there something that bothers us inherently about self-injury? Does it remind us of that most unfathomable of acts, suicide? Is self-injury just suicide by increments?

---

10 And the numbers we do have are likely skewed; self-injurers tend to cover up the behavior, so it is likely that the statistics we do have are lower than actual rates of occurrence.

Toward the end of the shootout at the OK Corral, Doc takes aim at Frank McLaury. Doc is an excellent shot—and fast, faster than McLaury on a good day—and now the man is likely mortally wounded. Doc finds the shot. He pulls the trigger.

The chamber clicks; the gun is empty.

McLaury laughs as well as a man with a bullet in his gut can. "I've got you now, you son of a bitch."

Doc spreads his arms out in a crucifixion pose. He is in precisely the least desirable position you want to take if a man aims to shoot you; he is as broad and exposed as possible.

Doc inclines his head. He is smiling. "You're a daisy if you do."

Chapter Eight: Lieutenant Tom Kazansky / Self-Regulation

Current mood: Busy

"[You're my problem.] You're *everyone's* problem. Every time you go up in the air, you're unsafe. I don't like you because you're dangerous."

—Lieutenant Tom "Iceman" Kazansky, *Top Gun*

Even when you're on a cocktail that works, you still have bipolar disorder. There are still symptoms. You are still a crazy person; you are still dangerous.

And even if you're completely asymptomatic, which is incredibly rare, your brain is still wired for bipolar disorder. You're still a silent film actor trying to make it in a Technicolor world. So how do you fill the gap?

Well, there's therapy. But mental health professionals generally have one mode with bipolar patients: drug and release. (In this, we're not unlike polar bears. Grrrr.)

In addition to that, unless you're much richer than I am, a therapist will not be following you around 24/7. So even if you find one who is really willing to work with you beyond tranq'ing and letting you back into the wild to fend for yourself, you're still going to be alone with your crazy at least some of the time. So what's the answer? How do you keep from being dangerous?

As in all things, it's best to rely on yourself.

When I say "dangerous," I mostly mean, "in danger of being sicker than you need to be," or sometimes, "a danger to yourself." Not so much, "in danger of being on the eleven o'clock news," though in rare cases, that does happen. Just like it does with sane people.

Anyway, the best way to keep from being dangerous is self-regulation. You have to be in charge of your disease.

The Kilmer Cure's Guide to Self-Regulation

- **You are not your disease.** It's important to remember that your disease is something that happened to you. It is not a defining feature of your personality, and it does not govern you.
- **You have a life outside bipolar disorder.** You have to live with this disease, but you do not have to live *for* this disease. It is okay to try new things, even if you don't know how your disease will react. It is *not* okay to define life through bipolar disorder's language. You can be happy or sad without being manic or depressed.
- **You can control this.** If something is going to trigger mania, don't do it. If something will make you so anxious that you will want to SI, don't do it. Avoid things that aggravate your disease. It's just like asthma or lupus: there are things that will cause flare-ups, and it's okay to avoid those things for your mental health.

In 1986, Val made a movie called *Top Gun*, which is about frat boys being irresponsible with seriously expensive government property. The protagonist, played by Tom Cruise, is Pete "Maverick" Mitchell—the writers decided to go with subtlety—whose every action is focused on bucking tradition and sticking it to the memory of his dead father. Val plays Tom "Iceman" Kazansky, Maverick's counterpoint. Ice is calm and disciplined; he obeys the rules and believes that the military is a team sport, and when you put an "I" in team, people get killed.

But Ice's demeanor is less personality than it is purposeful restraint. The man is tightly wound, but he's wound himself.

Ice has many of Maverick's personality traits—the irreverence, the cockiness, the attitude. The difference is that Ice also keeps himself in check when he's on the job. The same man who flies, "ice cold, no mistakes" snaps his teeth—literally—at Maverick when they're on the ground. He disrupts class to call Maverick on his bullshit, but when it's time to work he reins himself in. When it's time to work, he goes by the book and flies ice cold fucking perfect; this self-discipline is what separates him from Maverick.

If you want to be healthy while living with your disease, you cannot be Maverick. You have to be Ice. Maybe it isn't fair—okay, it *definitely* isn't fair. Sane people don't have to keep such a leash on themselves. Sane people do not have to make considerations for things like, "If I have a drink, will it trigger depression? Will it interact badly with my meds?" or "If I go to bed at 3 a.m., will I be manic tomorrow?" And it sucks that you do, but ignoring that you have a medical condition, a health problem that you need to manage, is just dumb. Sure, it's more fun to be Maverick, giving the finger to the world and doing whatever you want, regardless of the consequences, but Maverick does not have a chronic illness. (Also, he does end up getting his best friend killed. So there's that.) For longevity and good health: Team Iceman all the way.

Chapter Nine:
Frank Cavanaugh / Insomnia

Current mood: Awake

It is 3:30 a.m. I went to bed at nine thirty; I have to be up for class in three hours.

I have not had a single minute of sleep.

Sane people are such pussies when it comes to sleep. "Oh, I didn't get my eight hours last night; I just can't function today."

I haven't had a full night's sleep in 10 years. Sometimes I go weeks without any sleep, period.

You can go a long, long time before not sleeping will kill you. In the meantime, you just feel dead.

Zombie living.

The depressed insomniac is the walking dead. Actually the supine dead; the side effect is you spend a lot of time staring at your ceiling. Dear God; dear Buddha; dear Minka Aire, maker of my ceiling fan. Why aren't I asleep? In Ancient Greece, they reserved this kind of torture for people who stole fire from the gods. In this instance, it seems extreme.

The manic insomniac is Superman. I have no need for your puny Earthling notions of sleep. I have a carburetor to build! I have things to take apart and things to paint and things to build with my bare hands, despite having no idea of how they work. I can sleep when I'm dead.

In 2003, Val made the film *Blind Horizon.* Val plays the protagonist, a man named Frank Cavanaugh. Frank has some problems. He's lost his memory. Someone's trying to kill him. Someone's trying to kill the president, and only he knows about it, but no one believes him.

To top it all off, he can't sleep.

Frank spends the first part of *Blind Horizon* sleeping; he's in a coma. I don't know where this whole *after you wake up from a coma you never need sleep again* thing comes from, or if it's based in fact—judging from the rest of the medicine in this film, I'd guess no—but as tropes go, it annoys me almost as much as, say, amnesia. I kid. I actually like this movie; it's one of my favorites for when I have insomnia, myself.

Which is often.

Sleep disturbance is part of the diagnostic criteria for bipolar disorder. It can go either way; you can sleep more than normal people, or less.

During depression, some people sleep more than sixteen hours a day. Meanwhile, their mania is marked by bouts of high-energy, *I don't need sleep, I can sleep when I'm dead* insomnia, in which they get a lot of things done.

I generally have insomnia regardless of where I am in the bipolar cycle. There's the manic insomnia, where you're awake because you aren't tired, and there is the depressive insomnia, where you are awake despite being so tired your bones hurt.

During manic insomnia, you are a productive member of society. During depressive insomnia, there are basically three different routes you can travel:

- **The *I'm Totally Going to Sleep* Route** In this approach, you spend your sleepless hours doing everything you can to go to sleep. You drink warm milk; you count sheep. You attempt meditation for the first time in your life. You do all the stupid, self-help stuff you've ever heard Dr. Oz recommend.

- **The *Oh, God, Why Me?* Route** In this approach, you basically spend all night tossing, turning, and staring at your ceiling. You do everything you'd do in bed short of actually sleeping. You actively curse your alarm clock, and do constant mental math: how many minutes you have until you have to get up, unsated.
- **The *Fuck You, Insomnia* Route** In this approach, you act like you're awake on purpose. You get up, check your email. You get some homework or housework done. You watch television, cook, crochet. You pretend you are too good for sleep; this is just Daytime: Part Two.

Sadly, none of these things will result in a good night's sleep.

Chapter Ten: Madmartigan / Running on Automatic

Current mood: Drained

"Let me out of here, lend me a sword. I'll win this war for you."

—Madmartigan, *Willow*

In 1988, Val mad the film *Willow*, a fairytale piece in which an evil queen seeks to subvert a prophecy by killing a newborn child. Val plays Madmartigan, the irreverent outlaw reluctant hero that seems to be in every George Lucas movie. (Think Han Solo and Indiana Jones if you're unfamiliar with the type.)

Madmartigan is not crazy, but he's hardly fit to be left to his own devices. We first see him in a crow's cage, a hanging prison to which he's been sentenced for a reason never discussed (though we are led to believe it had something to do with sexual impropriety). He is manic and indulgent and easily distracted. He ruins every small task he's given.

Until you put a sword in his hand. Most of the time, Madmartigan cannot hold a thought in his head for two seconds, but on the field of battle, not only is he competent, he's brilliant—a specialist you can bring in to win a war. He goes from zero to kickass in a second flat, the moment you put him in his element.

My interest in Madmartigan's on/off switch is purely selfish. And no, for once I'm not talking about ogling half-naked Val Kilmer.

I work the same way. I can be in deep crazy, but there's one way to get me to competence. It's not a sword, though, I need thrust into my hands, but a pen. Or, more aptly, my computer.

When I write, even if I'm fully depressed or highly manic, I feel an internal calm. It's like something inside me switches to "on," and I can just run on automatic. It's a separate, competent part of myself.

Writing can be frustrating—sometimes it's work—but if I can tap into the automatic part, it's wonderful. It's the best I ever feel, like being a conduit for something grand. When it's automatic, I don't feel like I'm crafting something; I don't even feel like it's coming from me. I am unaware of the construction, the labor of writing, and yet I am more completely involved than anywhere else in my entire life.

Chapter Eleven: Chris Shiherlis / Treatment

Current mood: Grateful

In 1995, Val played a supporting role in the movie *Heat*. He shot the film at the same time he was filming *Batman Forever*. (He was also acting as a husband and father, and, if the former Mrs. Kilmer's divorce papers are to be believed, conducting an affair with a 20-year-old Drew Barrymore. I wish I had the man's time-management skills.)

Heat centers on the relationship between professional thief Neil McCauley (Robert De Niro) and the detective pursuing him, Lieutenant Vincent Hanna (Al Pacino). Val has a secondary role as a mechanic on McCauley's crew, a man named Chris Shiherlis. Val doesn't rack up much screen time, but Chris is key to understanding the film's central theme and internal morality.

Early on in the film, McCauley tells Chris, "Don't let yourself get attached to anything you are not willing to walk out on in 30 seconds flat if you feel the heat around the corner." This is McCauley's mantra, and he preaches it to the members of his crew; he also reveals it to Hanna. Hanna—who in fact *is* the heat—lives by a similar code; his work—his life as the heat—keeps him from becoming attached to anything, and he is constantly leaving his family to chase after bad guys. The film makes clear that McCauley's mantra is amoral. Chris ignores McCauley's mantra and instead lives for his wife, Charlene—"for me, my sun rises and sets with her," he says. Chris is the only member of McCauley's crew who makes it out of the movie alive. And he makes it out alive because two characters—his wife, Charlene, and McCauley himself, who thinks of Chris as a son—ignore McCauley's code, risking their own incarceration to save Chris's life.

One of the first things a therapist will ask you is what your support system is like. They're not talking about your bra, or an elaborate system of pulleys, though these are the things that spring immediately to mind every time I hear the phrase. (My brain naturally balks at psychobabble and the language of other soft sciences, I guess. Four years of physics and organic chemistry will do that to you.) A support system is the people in your life who you can count on to stick around and batten hatches and set up sandbags when Hurricane Crazy rolls into town. It can be composed of your friends, family, clergymen, or coworkers. And for the unfortunate few who have a dearth of those things, you're never completely without a support system: an integral part of your support system is your psychiatric team, the therapists and doctors overseeing your care.

The support system is a difficult concept for most people who have never been in treatment. Most sane people assume, upon being given a cursory explanation of the phrase, that it's just therapist-speak for "people you know." If asked for their own support system, they would hand over their Rolodex, or maybe a list of their Facebook friends. But the members of your support system have to be useful; they have to be willing to be active participants in your treatment. How many of your Facebook friends can you say that about?

The thing is, having a support system is not something normal people need to do. You have friends, you have family, you have coworkers. You have people you socialize with, and people who care about you. It's not necessary to have people actively participate in your treatment, because you're not *in* treatment.

A lot of being in treatment is coming to terms with the fact that you're not normal, and that you can't pretend otherwise. It's not really the 12-step, *the first step is admitting you have a problem* thing. It's that pretending to be normal will run counter to effective treatment. The problem here is that it's an adjustment. Most mental illnesses start during the teens and 20s, so basically you've been living your entire life sane, and then one day someone comes around and says, "Please forget everything you've spent your entire life learning and change all your habits, or you're going to get sicker and sicker until you die." It's rather like discovering, later in life, that you have a metabolic disorder. You take your medicine, you avoid certain behaviors, and you can live a long and healthy life managing your disease.

It sounds so easy; why would anyone buck treatment?

Nonadherence to treatment guidelines, especially medication regimens, is a problem for all medical issues; if you don't follow treatment, there isn't even a chance it will help you. Nonadherence by patients with mood disorders is especially high; some studies suggest nonadherence rates may be as high as 60 percent, meaning that for every 10 bipolar patients, six of them have bucked treatment at some point. That's a worse success rate than American marriages.

The reasons for nonadherence are myriad and complex. The number one predictor of whether a patient will buck treatment is the severity of the side effects from the medications they have been prescribed. There is a risk of side effects with every medication, but the side effects of psychiatric medications can be brutal, and even life threatening. The therapeutic/toxic ratio for lithium, one of the oldest and most-prescribed bipolar therapies, is very narrow (meaning that the amount of the drug you need to take for it to work, and the amount that will poison you, are very close together), and can be influenced by such benign activities as drinking water. Lithium users require frequent blood tests to monitor the level of the drug in their systems. Lithium can also cause massive weight gain, renal failure, and hypothyroidism. Antipsychotics like lithium can cause a condition called tardive dyskinesia, in which your body, particularly your face, moves often and without your involvement. This side effect is non-reversible; it will last you the rest of your life, even if you stop taking the medication. Drugs prescribed for bipolar disorder can cause hallucinations, depression, decreased coordination, liver damage, dizziness, memory loss, headache, arrhythmia, tremor, increased sensitivity to the sun, increased sensitivity to alcohol, increased risk of bone fractures, sexual dysfunction, muscle pain or weakness, blurred vision, anorexia, tachycardia, suicidal ideation, and anhedonia, the inability to feel pleasure.

Of course, side effects are only one reason for noncompliance. Money is often an issue; newer therapies can be hundreds of dollars for a single month's supply. And many medications, even if they are without side effects, take months to work, and it is easy to get discouraged when you're paying money for pills that seem to do nothing for you.

Bipolar disorder presents a particular problem. Mania can make you feel strong, smart, beautiful, invincible, *ecstatic*, and, although mania can be just as dangerous as depression, many bipolar patients will stop treatment simply to feel that high again.

I've bucked treatment because of side effects. And I've stopped taking my medications because they cost too much. But the reason I usually stop therapy is because I hate the feeling of being in therapy. Here's the pattern: my illness hits a nadir, and I think, "Holy fuck, I should be in treatment." Because, apparently, when things get bad enough, I get selective amnesia on top of my regular crazy, and completely forget the last time I quit treatment, and why. So I go back to treatment, and for a while I feel so good about myself, because I'm doing the right thing: I am committing to treatment. I am working the program. I am going to be sane and healthy and clean. I am going to live like normal people.

Forgetting that normal is not an option.

There is no endgame for treatment of bipolar disorder. Or, I guess, the endgame is the same as the treatment for any other chronic illness: you want to minimize the symptoms and lead as normal a life as possible. There is no tumor to excise. There is no gangrenous limb to remove. Despite my fervent, unwavering hopes, there is no part of me that can be cut out to make me well. It's like

Parkinson's, or Crohn's, or sickle cell. You have good days and bad days, but you always have the disease.

And that is how therapists and psychiatrists and social workers and doctors treat you: like you have a disease. Only a mental illness is not like a disease of the body, where there's something wrong with your lungs or there's something wrong with your diet, and you are just a reasonable person with a defect. When you're mentally ill, you are the defect; you are broken, fundamentally flawed, and you cannot be trusted with anything, not even your own treatment. You need a support system to make sure you don't fuck it all up.

I was 18 when I first went to therapy. My parents either didn't think I needed help, or didn't want to think I needed help, so my problems were never dealt with at home, never mentioned. I had to leave to get help; I first went to therapy after leaving for college. I went to the university counseling center, and spent two hours telling a stranger not much older than I was all the problems I'd had in the last six years, things I had never told anyone, things I hid under bandages and fake smiles and good grades.

She made me promise not to kill myself before I could come back for my next session, and gave me homework: a mood chart. A mood chart is exactly what it sounds like: a chart tracking changes in one's mood. The chart was in half-hour increments, and the method of indicating mood was color. The method of transferring the color to the page was coloring. With crayons.

Stay inside the lines. The lines are our friends. Apparently, I was both crazy and five years old.

I recognize that, for someone whose self-esteem is as low as mine, I have a very low threshold for people treating me badly. I also recognize that my 12-year-old therapist was not trying to insult my intelligence while applying her diagnostic tool. Still. This is mostly how I feel in therapy, like my doctors think I have brain damage. (Which, I guess . . . I kind of do. Hmm.) My therapists ask me if I understand the consequence of my actions, if I understand cause and effect. They ask me if I know what emotions are, what kind of emotions are produced under what circumstances?

"When do people feel happy?" "How did that make you feel?" "Do you understand you were having a natural emotion, there?" "Do you understand that people have different emotions?"

I stayed in treatment for 10 months the first time. It was group therapy that finally did me in; apparently, a meeting of the minds is only a good idea when it's sane minds. Leading a group of bipolar disorder patients is kind of like herding cats. Or leading a group of writers, I guess. Just imagine the worst workshop ever, and that's group therapy.

Two years passed before I went back into treatment. This time only lasted a few months. I stopped taking the medicine the doctor prescribed because it made me sick, depressed and anxious and hollow inside, and when I told the doctor, she told me I needed to quit school and check myself into the hospital. By which she meant a psychiatric hospital. An asylum. Clearly, this was not what I wanted to hear, so I told her I would take it under advisement. I then tore up the new prescriptions, and never went back.

Since then, I've been in and out of treatment several times. I could give you the blow-by-blow, but it's all pretty much the same. You decide you hate being crazy, and go to treatment. You then decide you hate treatment, and stop going. Lather, rinse, repeat.

While fleeing the bank job after Hanna makes them, Chris Shiherlis is shot in the chest. The force of the automatic weapon is enough to knock him to the ground. He falls. McCauley sees him on the ground; he is many yards away. They are surrounded by police, and Chris is in the thick of it, in the line of fire for at least one police officer, as the blood marring his shirt can attest. McCauley doesn't hesitate. He runs through the hail of bullets to where Chris is lying.

"Come on!" McCauley says, but Chris cannot stand on his own. McCauley shoulders his weapon so his hands are free to hoist Chris to his feet, so his hands are free to carry him.

Here's the thing. 60 percent of mood disorder patients buck treatment. Many of us do it over and over, like yo-yo dieting. We start treatment; we stop treatment. We start treatment; we stop treatment.

But as many times as we stop treatment, we always go back to it. Because being mentally ill is hard, but it's harder alone.

And sometimes you need someone to carry you.

Chapter Twelve: Perry van Shrike / Self-Loathing

Current mood: Shut up, brain

In 2005, Val made a film called *Kiss Kiss Bang Bang*. It is a difficult movie to classify; it meets the criteria of noir, but it also subverts the genre for laughs, so it's somewhere between an homage and a satire.

Val plays Perry van Shrike, called "Gay Perry" for the obvious reason. Gay Perry, in a subversion of noir's strict gender roles, is the most competent, badass character in the film.

He's also one of the funniest, with an acerbic humor usually aimed at Harry Lockhart, the film's protagonist.

PERRY: Jesus. Look up "idiot" in the dictionary, you know what you'll find?
HARRY: A picture of me?
PERRY: *No*, the definition of the word "idiot," which you *fucking are*!

`Perry van Shrike is not a man who suffers fools.`

In the vein of self-injury and suicidal ideation, self-loathing is a self-destructive fact of life for the bipolar patient. Self-loathing mostly goes with depression, but it can also pop up during mixed states and mania. It's even a problem when the patient is medicated, because by then it is a learned behavior.

Self-loathing is like having Perry van Shrike live in your head. It's not an external voice—that's schizophrenia—but your own, saying hateful things to you all the livelong day. You sit down to write a paper. Perry watches over your shoulder.

"Who the fuck are you to string two words together?"

"Shut up," you say, and begin to write. Perry waits until you make a mistake.

"Of all the dipshit things to do," he says. "Who taught you grammar?"

You tap irritably at the backspace key. "Sane people make mistakes."

"How you can claim to know that, given your vast experience with sanity, is beyond me," Perry says. "I can't believe you're doing this. Why don't you just go outside and step in front of a bus, instead?"

"Quiet, you."

You finish the paper, and print a copy to turn in. Perry watches you wrestle the stapler.

"I sure as shit hope you're better at collating than you are at, oh, anything else."

"I can't even collate in peace?"

"Apparently not, idiot," Perry says, and nods at the bead of blood welling up on your thumb. Stupid stapler.

And on it goes. You cannot even collate without your backseat driver critiquing everything that you do. At least with self-loathing, you're never self-lonely.

Chapter Thirteen: Ray Levoi / Passing

Current mood: Depressed

Cut to a very expensive, highly polished desk, and the file atop it, marked FEDERAL BUREAU OF INVESTIGATION. A manicured hand begins to flip through the file. Glossy black and white photographs are removed and spread over the desk. Pan up to Deputy Director William Dawes of the FBI.

DAWES

Levoi.

The door clicks closed, and we pan up. Entering the room is an intense, quiet young man, Special Agent Ray Levoi. He wears a standard issue government haircut and a suit—inexpensive, but well-fit; blue, not black.

There is something insatiable about him—a hungry energy that won't let him go.

Ray enters Dawes' office and starts toward the desk.

DAWES

Your name popped up this morning, Raymond. Impressive background. Two years street work, three years underground.

Ray has a seat before Dawes' desk.

DAWES

You've done some fine deep cover work.

RAY

Thank you, sir.

DAWES

How's the Colonel?

Ray smiles. Now that the conversation has struck a friendly tone, he unbuttons his suit jacket to facilitate crossing his legs.

RAY

My father's fine, sir. He sends his regards.

DAWES

He's a good man. I was just looking over your family tree, here.

Dawes glances down at the file in his lap—Ray's file.

DAWES

It's quite a mixture: Lithuanian, Scots-Irish, French—

Dawes looks up at Ray from over his glasses. He doesn't need to read this part.

DAWES

American Indian. Sioux Indian, isn't it?

Dawes removes his glasses, and studies Ray. Ray looks uncomfortable.

RAY

I, uh, don't know.

DAWES

Sioux. Your real father was half, isn't that right?

Ray looks shaken, and it takes him a moment to answer.

RAY

I didn't know my father, sir; he died when I was a baby.

DAWES

He died when you were seven.

Ray doesn't say anything, but he looks like he's been struck. He swallows, almost nods, the only response he can muster.

In 1992, Val Kilmer starred in *Thunderheart* (my very favorite Val Kilmer movie, for those of you playing the at-home version), a creative reimagining of the problems experienced by the American Indian Movement in the late 1970s. Val plays Special Agent Ray Levoi, an FBI agent who is chosen for an assignment in the

Badlands because his biological father—who died when Ray was a child, and whom he has long since buried in his psyche—was half Sioux.

Ray's stepfather is a military man, and well regarded by the FBI brass. Ray has essentially been passing all of his life, but at the end of the day, his stepfather may be one of the boys, but he isn't.

The moment his friends and colleagues at the FBI see a way they can use him—as a PR stunt, as a symbol, not as a person and certainly not as the "fine field agent" he has proven himself to be—they do it. They use him, and the place in the world Ray has spent his life crafting is destroyed.

Thunderheart is about many things, racial and political and spiritual things, but at its heart it is Ray's story, his story of finding his new place in the world now that he is no longer content to "pass."

Psychiatrists love diagnosing things. Sticking things in the proper Skinner boxes and slapping labels on them. It's surprisingly number-based, for a so-called "soft science"; perhaps the name has given them an inferiority complex. If Freud has taught us anything, it's that what you want to be, in all things, at all times, is *rock hard.* And so psychiatry employs a lot of charts and applies quantifiers and numbers to inquantifiable things like *I want to kill myself* and *There's no reason I should hurt but all I do is hurt.* Never let the abstract get in the way of the numbers.

Solid as a rock.

The DSM-IV, properly the Diagnostic and Statistical Manual of Mental Disorders (Fourth Edition), has numbers. Quotas. You do not qualify as a diagnosis without meeting its exacting criteria. "Diagnosis requires at least one hypomanic episode and at least one major depressive episode." Requires. Defined as "to have need of," "to call for or exact as obligatory." From the Latin requīrere, to search for again and again. To have an insatiable need for, such that you will scour the earth endlessly, like some damned thing. The headless horseman, the vengeful spirit—unable to move from this plane lacking that essential part.

For a discipline that makes so much of inadvertent verbal slips—I'm looking at you again, Freud—they are so careless with their language.

Most bipolar patients will not have a complete cycle within a year; they will not transition all the way from mania to depression and back within 12 months. The episodes are unpredictable, and they linger, lasting on average between three and six months. However, some patients have quicker cycles. The DSM-IV, and its insatiable lust for quantifying, has taken notice of this. Patients having four or more episodes a year—major depressive, manic, hypomanic, or mixed episodes; the DSM-IV cares about numbers, not quality of life—are called "rapid cycling." There are variations on this theme. Ultra-rapid, ultra-ultra rapid, ultradian cycling. It sounds like a list from the feminine hygiene aisle, which is perhaps fair.

I've given a lot of thought to the subject of passing. Though we are long past the days where "institutionalization" meant "locking you up and throwing away the key," there is still enormous stigma attached to mental illness. As PC as modern American society is, it's still commonplace—acceptable—to make slurs about the mentally ill. People say, "Oh, you know me; I'm so crazy!" You're not crazy. You're wacky, maybe, or zany, or maybe you have a unique fashion sense or can't hold your liquor. You're not crazy. I'm crazy. Will you be on medication the rest of your life? Do you fantasize about killing yourself? No? Then you're not fucking crazy, so stop saying it.

"Bipolar," specifically, is often used. Anyone whose keel isn't even gets the kneejerk, "Oh, Jimmy is so bipolar sometimes." Jimmy is moody; maybe Jimmy's an asshole. Jimmy is not bipolar; stop saying it.

"What's the big deal?" you say. "They're only words." "Sticks and stones may break my bones but words can never hurt me." The problem is, language like this is indicative of a dichotomy. On the one hand, you have normal life: sanity. On the other, you have an aberration, the bad thing: mental illness. The thing is, the default assumption is that you're sane. Bipolar disorder is a silent illness; it isn't like blindness or polio, where people can just look at you and tell. They assume you're "normal"—read, sane—until proven otherwise.

So you pass, until someone says something. Until someone says that they're crazy for wearing white after Labor Day, or says something ignorant like people with mental illnesses don't need drugs; they just need to think positively. And then, maybe you can't keep your big mouth shut, and everybody knows your secret.

Or maybe you can keep your mouth shut, and you sit there, persecuted and hunted, an aberration. But passing.

My friend Carla, who also has bipolar disorder, has a thing for werewolves.

"It's like us, honey," she rasps, her dark honey voice. She is competent and confident and beautiful, and as long as I've known her—many years now—I have always felt like her little sister. Loved and loving and awed. "We look normal, but inside there's this terrible transformation. Something we can't control; something that happens to us."

We are sisters in this, I suppose. A pack.

Mostly I pass. Have you ever done something wrong, and gotten away with it? And there's this rush, this sudden, giddy realization that it is so, so easy. (Giddy means "lighthearted," but it also means "dizzy.") That's how I feel, passing. It should be this great trial, pretending to be another person, a different kind of person—pretending to be normal and happy when inside you are lit up with pain. But it isn't. It's easy—not like breathing, but a no-brakes, out of control kind of easy. A slippery easy. And most people are so wrapped up in their own shit that they have no time to think about yours, so pretending to be sane is the easiest game in town.

Until it isn't.

"Something that happens to us," Carla says. "Something we can't control." And sometimes I can't control it. Sometimes it takes over me, like an exorcism.

RAY:

Listen. I'm not who you think I am. I'm sorry.

I've lost my insurance again, which means I've been off my meds since November, which means things are worse than usual. Closer to the surface. At first things were okay; I was really surprised, in fact, by how fine I was doing. Until I was setting my alarm for an hour before I needed to get up so I would have time to self-injure before class; until I wasn't leaving the house unless doing so was absolutely necessary. When things are good, they're fine, but when they're bad, baby, they're *bad*. Bipolar disorder doesn't do things in half measures. Whether you're high or low, it's balls to the wall, full force, no brakes.

Last week, I went out with some friends to a local bar. Being in public, being social, is hard for me even if it's people I really like, and it had been a bad week.

In the literary world, we call this foreshadowing.

Mood exists on a spectrum; everything is connected. You have to be careful with your meds—if you correct too much for mania, you can cause depression; if you take too much antidepressant, you can cause mania. Of course, your psychiatric medication isn't the only thing that can affect mood. Other substances, other drugs, can affect it. Even behavior, situation, can change things.

I was with my friends; I was having a good time. I was living like normal people live. And then the full moon rose, and I was exposed.

Sometimes, when I'm really high, emotion-wise, I will all of a sudden crash. Hard. Usually it presents this way: in the middle of laughing, I will suddenly be hit with a tidal wave of sadness. I start sobbing, so hard I can't breathe, so hard my muscles go weak; I can't control my body. This is called a mixed state, and it is a feature of rapid cycling. Basically, you are having a manic episode *and* a depressive episode, both at the same time.

It is a spectacular showcase of insanity.

And my latest one was in public—not just in front of my friends, but in front of an entire tavern full of people. In a few seconds, without warning, I was different in everyone's eyes forever. I had stopped passing.

Passing. As I've said, I have been giving a lot of thought to the subject. I've also been giving a lot of thought to the term itself; I'm a writer, and I like words. I like to know how they work. As euphemisms go, "passing" is fairly benign, but I hate it. As analogies go, it's gross. What do we pass? The buck. Pass the buck. We pass money—counterfeit money. When you *pass*, it's like saying you're not genuine. Like being white, or straight, or sane—that's genuine. And if you're not that, you're fake. You're not real.

I want to be real.

Sometimes I don't feel real. I feel empty, a shell full of sticky scratchy insulation—something manmade, mostly air. When what you are exists only as a counterpoint to the norm, how can you feel real?

Chapter Fourteen: Robby Gallagher / Isolation

Current Mood: Lonely

In 2000, Val made the film *Red Planet*. He plays NASA mechanical systems engineer Robby Gallagher, part of a team of astronauts sent to Mars to ready the planet for earthling habitation. Predictably, things go horribly awry, and by the film's end, Robby is the only person left alive on the unforgiving red planet.

As a suggested therapy, I've been trying affirmations to combat negative thoughts. For instance: bipolar brain thinks *God, I'm so ugly*; you strike back with the positive affirmation, *I am beautiful*. I'm not very good at them—*I am excellent at affirmations*—but I have been doing them often enough to notice trends. The affirmations I use most often have to do with social acceptance. *People like me. No one is judging me. I am loved.* Mental illnesses are isolating; you live in your head, and sometimes it's difficult to travel outside your head into the real world. There's mental jet lag, and things between you and the natives of the real world can get lost in translation. And let's not forget self-loathing. With all this, interpersonal relationships for the bipolar patient can be extremely challenging.

And then there's another kind of isolation.

It is April 20, 2012, and two weeks ago, I was in what they call the crisis or 48-hour ward of what you would probably call a mental hospital, what they used to call an insane asylum or a loony bin. (Booby hatch? Nut house? Cuckoo's nest?) "This is like a psychiatric emergency room," said the doctor on call, an MD and not a psychiatrist. He also told me I was not the kind of patient he was used to seeing there, in such a way that I was reminded of that scene in *Lady and the Tramp*, where Lady is rescued from the pound and told that she is much too nice a girl to be in a place like that.

It was April, and I had been off my meds for six months. April showers bring May flowers. I wasn't going to make it to May.

You reach a point in the thick of depression, where suicidal ideation reaches its head and the pain kind of breaks, and there's a calm. There is an eerie sort of stillness, because you have decided that you are going to kill yourself and you have crafted a plan, and there is something so fucking comforting and stable in that, amid the chaos of your unsound mind, something steady to hold onto. It feels sane.

I went to the emergency room. There was a sign-in sheet, and I wrote my name and my date of birth, and on the line that said *reason for visit* I wrote *suicidal ideation*. Technically I checked myself into the hospital, but after I wrote down the word *suicide*, I became what the state calls a *10-13*. This means that I lost my decision making privileges until medical personnel decided I was no longer a threat to myself or others. I did not get to leave until they said so.

Which was over 30 hours later, and I had to be released into the custody of an upstanding member of the community, like I was getting out of rehab. And I have people who love me, people who will come and pick me up from mental hospitals and then take me to get Chinese food, people who will look after my dogs and leave me voicemail messages saying I don't have to call them back, they just want me to know that they are thinking about me.

But I don't have anyone who knows what it's like to have to relinquish your shoelaces for fear you might hang yourself with them. Or anyone who's ridden in the back of a police car, because state law mandates that 10-13s be transferred by cruiser or ambulance, and I don't have insurance, so the burden fell on the state.

("I'm supposed to cuff you," the cop said, unsmiling, "but if you promise not to give me any trouble, we can skip it." I looked at him—a foot taller than me, a hundred pounds heavier, and covered in weapons—and wanted to say, "Exactly what kind of trouble are you expecting, officer?" but managed to contain myself, as I did not wish to be tazed.)

I don't have anyone who has this thing living inside them, this *Thanatos* monster that makes all these hellish things necessary. And so even when I am surrounded by people, sometimes I am still completely isolated.

Robby Gallagher sits in the alkaline dust of the red planet, listening to the breathing of Kate Bowman—his commander and almost-lover—through his headset. She is stuck on the space station orbiting the planet, an atmosphere away, indistinguishable by sight from the stars speckling the inky sky. He has 30 seconds left to speak with her, before orbit and batteries and the fates conspiring against them drops their comm connection.

"I, uh, really hate this planet," Robby says, squinting into the night. "I really miss Earth. I really miss a lot of things. I, uh, I'm gonna miss you." Silence filters across the line. Maybe he's out of time. "Aren't you gonna say anything? I should have kissed you."

Finally, a reply. "Yeah," Kate says. "You should have kissed me."

The line goes dead; time is up. He is now good and truly alone.

Chapter Fifteen: Simon Templar / The Real Me

Current mood: Ambivalent

In 1997, Val made a film called *The Saint*. The movie was an adaptation of a series of novels by British author Leslie Charteris. It's very popular abroad, but I hadn't heard of *The Saint* or its protagonist, Simon Templar, until I saw this movie. In addition to the novels, there have been many radio, film, television, and graphic interpretations of the books. Simon was even played by Roger Moore, whom you probably know as Bond, James Bond.

Val plays the Saint himself, Simon Templar. Simon's life of crime began early; he used his quick mind and his good hands to pick locks and filch extra food in the orphanage where he was raised. Stealing is his only real talent—okay, stealing and romancing women are his only real talents, but the film is rated PG-13, so guess which one he does for a living.

Simon's got a fun job, a plush bank account, and scores of adoring women; life should be peachy. But he's also got a problem. The saints.

Simon's job is highly illegal and usually not terribly subtle, so instead of going around as himself, he uses a myriad of disguises, all named and modeled after Catholic saints. The trouble is, he never seems to have the occasion to be himself. Always, he is somebody else.

What Simon really needs is a shrink, but in the film he settles for lonely hearts nuclear physicist Emma Russell, a person with whom he can finally be himself.

Integration is the act of combining disparate pieces into an integrated whole. In psychology, integration is usually associated with success in dissociative identity disorder—not bipolar disorder—but I think that's part of the drug-and-release modus operandi adopted by most mental health practitioners in response to bipolar disorder. Shouldn't integration be our concern, too? We have these separate cycles, like a werewolf's phases; we have these two people, the Sane Me and the Crazy Me. Shouldn't we work on making our halves into wholes?

One girl, two moods. Maybe what I need isn't mood stabilizers and antidepressants, these chemicals that alter how I naturally feel; maybe what I need is to get good with feeling everything. Maybe what I need is just to get good with being myself.

Of course, then the question becomes: who am I? How much of this is bipolar disorder, and how much of it is me? I don't remember how normal feels, how I am without bipolar disorder, and even when I'm on drugs, I'm just that: bipolar and on drugs. What parts of me are intrinsic, and what parts are the disease? There's the Sane Me and the Crazy Me; who is the Real Me?

Chapter Sixteen: Scott / In-Treatment

Current mood: Blah

"You're gonna take this fight to bed with you for a long time. You don't gotta do it all tonight."

—Scott, *Spartan*

In 2004, Val starred in David Mamet's *Spartan,* a film about a special operative who is brought in to handle the most sensitive of situations. Val's Army Ranger Scott is given a task: to find a girl who has gone missing. What he finds is that the people handling him are doing just that—*handling* him. He finds that sometimes you cannot trust anyone but yourself. One riot, one Ranger.

My friend Chantel picks me up from the hospital in her hand-me-down Jaguar with Florida plates. The sun setting over a peaceful ocean; a manatee floating above the water, as if touched by Tinkerbell's magic fairy dust. *Think happy thoughts.* Two days later, I am sitting in a therapist's office looking at finger paint and crayon scribble depictions of children's ideas of a happy life. There are a few unicorns, and an eleven-fingered man clutching a bundle of cash. Because I don't have insurance, the doctor at the hospital has sent me to a place called Gateway, a government-funded agency with sliding-scale mental health services. They also do a lot of addiction recovery stuff, and the waiting room was full of people awaiting their Crystal Meth Anonymous meeting.

My therapist's name is Melody or Melinda or Melanie, and she has lank brown hair and long, pale fingers. She looks maybe five years older than I am. She talks at me looking at her computer screen; I talk to her looking at the crayon utopias on her wall. At the end of the visit, she gives me the paperwork I need to give my college's counseling offices before I'm allowed to go back to class, the sanity hoops I have to jump through to prove I'm not a danger to myself and others—a preemptive strike against litigation, I am sure. Part of the paperwork is the DSM's five axes. The first four axes are stuff I know—my diagnosis, extenuating factors, etc. The fifth and final axis, though, is new to me, a window into her assessment of me. *Global Assessment of Functioning is for reporting the clinician's judgment of the individual's overall level of functioning. This information is useful in planning treatment and measuring its impact, and in predicting outcome.* It's a scale of 1 (very bad) to 100 (very good). She put me down as a 55.

That bitch.

The girl is sick. She sits at the edge of the chair, curling into herself like a crustacean. "Did my father send you?" she says. She may be crying now. "One man."

"One riot, one Ranger," Scott says. "You ever heard that?"

"Leonidas," she says, "king of Sparta. When a neighboring state would plead for military aid, would send one man."

"Well," Scott says, "there you go."

Epilogue: Dear Val

Dear Val,

I have been on my meds for eleven months. It is almost a year since Chantel picked me up from the hospital—me with no shoelaces, her in her hand-me-down Jaguar with the Florida manatee plates—almost a year since the last time I tried to kill myself.

It's not perfect. There are gaps, things that are probably symptoms peeking through the meds, but that might just be me. I'll never be sure what's just me, and what's the disease. I get nervous driving, for instance; gruesome scenes of fire and twisted metal pop into my head every time someone inches too close to my bumper or changes lanes without signaling. And I still sometimes think, "I'm going to kill myself" when I don't feel well, but the thought just slides off like butter across a hot pan. It's an empty threat with no teeth.

It's been a while, honestly, since I watched one of your movies. I still love them, of course; I just don't need them anymore. They're no longer my project; I no longer need projects. Your movies aren't keeping me alive anymore, because me and the drugs, we're keeping me alive now. It's kind of weird not to miss you. A couple days after I got out of the hospital, I got a tattoo on my arm—somewhere I could always see it—that says, "Sometimes life forces us to defend ourselves." It's a quote from Joseph M. Marshall III's *The Lakota Way*. I remember lying on the middle school gym mat that served as a bed in the hospital, and feeling more alone than I ever had in my whole life, and wishing for *something* to hold onto. So I got this tattoo, so I would never be alone again; I would always have that, my mantra, my koan. And I feel the same way about you as I do, now, when I look at that tattoo. It's something I needed once, but I feel divorced from that time and place, like it wasn't even me that was there. Like it's a story from a movie I've seen many times, so many times I can imagine myself in the role.

I don't live there anymore.

In therapy, we call this progress.

I'm doing well.

Works Cited

American Psychological Association. *Diagnostic and Statistical Manual of Mental Disorders.* 4th ed. Washington, D.C.: American Psychological Association, 1994. Print.

Batman Forever. Dir. Joel Schumacher. Warner Bros., 1995. DVD.

Blind Horizon. Dir. Michael Haussman. Lions Gate, 2005. DVD.

Burgess, Wes. The Bipolar Handbook: Real-Life Questions with Up-to-Date Answers. New York: Avery, 2006.

Fight Club. Dir. David Fincher. 20th Century Fox, 1999. DVD.

Head, Steve. "Interview with Val Kilmer." IGN.com: April 29, 2002. Online.

Heat. Dir. Michael Mann. Warner Bros., 1995. DVD.

The Island of Dr. Moreau. Dir. John Frankenheimer. New Line Cinema, 1996. DVD.

Kill Me Again. Dir. John Dahl. MGM, 1989. DVD.

Kiss Kiss Bang Bang. Dir. Shane Black. Warner Bros., 2005. DVD.

Red Planet. Dir. Antony Hoffman. Village Roadshow Pictures, 2000. DVD.

Saint, The. Dir. Phillip Noyce. Paramount Pictures, 1997. DVD.

Salton Sea, The. Dir. D.J. Caruso. Warner Bros., 2002. DVD.

Spartan. Dir. David Mamet. Warner Bros., 2004. DVD.

Thunderheart. Dir. Michael Apted. Tristar Pictures, 1992. DVD.

Tombstone. Dir. George P. Cosmatos. Buena Vista Pictures, 1993. DVD.

Top Gun. Dir. Tony Scott. Paramount Pictures, 1986. DVD.

Willow. Dir. Ron Howard. Lucasfilm, 1988. DVD.

Appendix A: Medication

Let's talk about drugs.

Drugs are a fact of life for the bipolar patient. I have said it before, but mental health professionals basically have one mode with bipolar patients: drug and release. If you are going to be in treatment, you will be in treatment your whole life. And this means being on drugs for your whole life.

This would be fine, if being on psych meds was like popping a daily low-dose aspirin: good for you, and with minimum side effects.

It isn't.

Even when they're working properly and you're taking them exactly how you should, psych meds have an enormous number of side effects. I've lost weight, gained weight. I've gone weeks without sleeping, and then they put you on sleeping meds and you still can't sleep, so you're just the walking dead. Depakote made me feel nothing. Cymbalta made me feel so much—everything—that I had to be tranquilized.

If you are going to be in treatment, you will be in treatment your whole life.

This means being on drugs for your whole life.

The basic approach to medicating the bipolar patient is two-pronged. First, a doctor will put the patient on a medication called a mood-stabilizer. That sounds like it would be enough of a cure all on its own—the problem of bipolar disorder is unstable moods—but in reality, a mood-stabilizer only counteracts mania.

Once the patient has been on a mood stabilizer for a week or two, the doctor will add a drug to battle depression, the more aptly named "antidepressant." There are several different kinds of antidepressants, but they all work on one (or more) of three chemicals in the brain called "monoamine neurotransmitters": serotonin (sometimes called 5-HT or "the happiness hormone"), norepinephrine (sometimes called noradrenaline), and dopamine (for some reason, always called dopamine).

After the patient is steady on their cocktail, the psychiatrist may add additional drugs for things like anxiety and sleep, or to counteract side effects of the first two medications. The basic game plan, though, is mood-stabilizer plus antidepressant.

Before you can understand how psychotropic drugs work, you have to understand a few things about how the brain works.

The basic operating unit of the brain is called a neuron. A neuron is made up of three main parts: the cell body, called the soma; and the axon and dendrite, which are kinds of arms extending from the cell body. Neurons inside the central nervous system are packed tightly, but there is always a space between the axon and the dendrite of neighboring cells (neurons are packed axon to dendrite, not axon to axon, like the positive and negative ends of batteries); this space is called the synapse.

The synapse is where communication between neurons happens. There are two types of communication: electrical and chemical. Electrical communication is controlled by sodium channels. I know what you're thinking: sodium is salt; isn't that chemical? The explanation is complicated, so just go with it. All you need to know is that electrical communication between neurons is controlled by sodium channels. Chemical communication between neurons is controlled by chemicals called neurotransmitters. There are several different types of neurotransmitters, but the ones important to bipolar medications are called monoamine neurotransmitters. They are serotonin, norepinephrine, and dopamine.

Changes in any part of neuron-to-neuron communication—be it electrical changes in the sodium channels, or chemical changes to neurotransmitters—can change mood and behavior.

Let's do things in order, and talk about mood stabilizers first.

Mood-Stabilizers

There are several different kinds of mood-stabilizers: lithium, anticonvulsants, and antipsychotics. "Mood-stabilizer" as a term describes what the medication does, not how it functions, so we'll describe each category in turn.

Mood-Stabilizers: Lithium

Lithium was first used to treat bipolar disorder in the first half of the 20th-century, and it remains a popular mood stabilizer today. Lithium is an element that occurs naturally in the earth; lithium as a medication is a salt form of the element lithium.

In chemistry, the efficacy of drugs is sometimes measured in percentages. There are two important percentages to medications: efficacy level and toxicity level. The first is the percentage of drug to kilograms of patient is necessary for the drug to work; the second is how much of the drug you can have in your system before the drug becomes a poison. The efficacy and toxicity levels of lithium are very close to one another, which means that being on lithium requires constant blood tests to monitor lithium levels in the patient's bloodstream.

But what doesn't kill you makes you stronger. Almost poisoning you is just one of many side effects of lithium. Lithium can cause weight gain, increased appetite and thirst, diabetes, and involuntary eye movements. It can cause hypothyroidism (reduced activity of the thyroid gland) and may affect the function of the kidneys.

Mood-Stabilizers: Anticonvulsants

Anticonvulsants are drugs traditionally prescribed to epileptics to control seizures, but in the last few decades, their uses have expanded to everything from preventing migraine headaches to treating neuropathy (nerve pain and tingling, usually in the extremities). The term anticonvulsant, too, describes the effect of the medication and not the method of action, so no specific mechanism can be described. Anticonvulsants popularly used as mood-stabilizers include Depakote, Lamictal, Tegretol, and Trileptal.

Depakote is a salt. Depakote works by affecting the transmission of the neurotransmitter GABA. Side effects include hallucinations, decreased coordination, and liver damage.

Lamictal is the only other medication (besides lithium) approved by the FDA as a mood-stabilizer. It works by stopping the release of several amino acids that work within the brain. Its side effects include dizziness, lack of coordination, memory loss, meningitis, and life-threatening skin conditions like Stevens-Johnson syndrome, in which cell death causes the epidermis to separate from the dermis (which sounds kind of benign, but is in reality Cronenberg-levels of horrifying).

Tegretol works on electrical, not chemical communication between neurons by closing sodium channels in the brain. Like lithium, it requires constant blood tests, because the medication can lower white cell count in the bloodstream. It is one of the only mood-stabilizers that is relatively safe to use during pregnancy, but it has a very high potential for negative drug interactions. Side effects include headache, arrhythmia, and motor coordination impairment. Tegretol can also greatly decrease the patient's ability to tolerate alcohol.

Trileptal is a chemical relative of Tegretol, and works similarly while not exposing patients to the lowering of white blood cells possible with Tegretol. However, Trileptal is not safe to take during pregnancy. Its side effects include headache, tremor, and increased sensitivity to the sun.

Mood-Stabilizers: Antipsychotics

To your face, a doctor will call these drugs "mood-stabilizers," but really, they're antipsychotics. This is the same medicine they give to people with schizophrenia to calm them down. They are sedatives.

And they are sedatives with terrifying side effects. The metabolism is affected; patients gain so much weight, and are unable to shed it, that often that is their sole reason for dumping the drug. It's a choice between being fat and well or thin and sick. Insomnia, sexual dysfunction, anxiety, sleeplessness. Shaking, nausea, vomiting, swelling, cramps, dizziness.

And then there's the big one. The big side effect—the trademark of antipsychotics—is called tardive dyskinesia. Tardive dyskinesia is a movement disorder in which your body moves repetitively and without your involvement. Your body moves without your permission, and it does it all the time. You cannot not move. The movements are usually in the face, mouth, and jaw; Heath Ledger's Joker in *The Dark Knight* has tardive dyskinesia.

Atypical antipsychotics are so-called because they were developed specifically to make patients less at risk for tardive dyskinesia than the original ("typical") antipsychotics. But studies suggest that, after sustained use, being on any kind of antipsychotic will likely result in tardive dyskinesia.

And, if you stay in treatment, you will be on drugs for your whole life.

Antidepressants

Antidepressants fall into several basic categories: MAOIs (monoamine oxidase inhibitors), tricyclic antidepressants, SSRIs (selective-serotonin reuptake inhibitors), and SNRIs (serotonin-norepinephrine reputake inhibitors). What they all have in common is they work on three chemicals in the brain called monoamine neurotransmitters: serotonin, norepinephrine, and dopamine.

Antidepressants: MAOIs

MAOIs are among the first antidepressants, but today they are rarely used, because they interact negatively with many other medications and even some foods, and because their method of action is so broad. MAOIs work by inhibiting a brain chemical called monoamine oxidase. Monoamine oxidase is responsible for the breakdown of monoamine neurotransmitters; if the neurotransmitters are not broken down by monoamine oxidase, this means there are more of them available in the brain.

Unfortunately, MAOIs can react fatally with a myriad of drugs and foods containing the amino acid tyramine (most notably pork, cheese, and chocolate).

Antidepressants: SSRIs

"SSRI" stands for "selective-serotonin reuptake inhibitor." Normally, when neurotransmitters like serotonin are released in the brain, they are then collected by a "reuptake protein" and broken down. Basically, the reuptake protein packs the neurotransmitter up until the next time it is to be used; this is called "reuptake." SSRIs stop this process for selected—that is, not every kind—of serotonin molecules. SSRIs include Celexa, Lexapro, Prozac, Paxil, and Zoloft. Side effects include anhedonia, somnolence, fatigue, insomnia, increased risk of bone fractures, sexual dysfunction, and suicidal ideation.

Antidepressants: SNRIs

SNRIs work similarly to SSRIs, though they stop the reuptake of both serotonin and norepinephrine; basically they make it so that, instead of being put away neatly, these chemicals slosh around in your brain, getting used over and over again.

SNRIs are antidepressants; their job is to elevate mood. Doctors will always start bipolar patients on a mood stabilizer before putting them on an antidepressant, even if they are suicidal, because an antidepressant can raise the mood too much, causing mania. Ironically, antidepressants can also cause *increased* depression; Some patients, especially younger people, report increased suicidal ideation following the start of an Effexor or other antidepressant regimen.

Because serotonin and norepinephrine work in a lot of different body systems, drugs like Effexor have a lot of side effects. The most common are things like nausea and somnolence (feeling sleepy all the time), but there are also instances of things like muscle pain or weakness, blurred vision, anorexia, tachycardia (elevated heart rate), and tremor.

Antidepressants: Tricyclic Antidepressants

Tricyclic antidepressants work similarly to SNRIs, stopping the "reuptake" of the brain chemicals serotonin and norepinephrine. Side effects include anhedonia, blurred vision, sexual dysfunction, and irregular heart rhythm. Tricyclic antidepressants are more likely than SNRIs to cause heart problems, and patients are more likely to become tolerant to them than with SNRIs.

Antidepressants as a whole have two major side effects that cause patients to buck treatment. The first is weight gain. Use of antidepressants usually causes weight gain between 10 and 50 pounds, but can sometimes cause gains of more than 100 pounds. Antidepressants cause increased cravings and low energy levels; additionally, serotonin is involved in telling the body when it has had enough to eat, and the manipulation of the neurotransmitter by antidepressants can cause it to fail in this job.

The second major side effect of antidepressants is low sex drive and sexual dysfunction. This side effect can manifest in a number of ways, from complete deadening of the libido to inability to orgasm to inability to feel emotions of romantic attachment; antidepressants can keep you from falling in love.

Appendix B: Glossary of Terms

10-13

Hospital code for "hold patient for psychiatric evaluation." Involuntary committal to emergency psychiatric care of a patient who staff believes is a danger to themselves or others.

Anhedonia

The inability to feel pleasure, often a symptom of depression or the medications used to treat it.

Antidepressant

A drug used to combat depression and otherwise "lift" mood.

Antipsychotic

A drug used to combat psychosis in schizophrenics and mania in bipolar patients. See also: mood stabilizer.

Barrymore, Drew

Child star made good, Drew Barrymore is an American actress, model, writer, and director. At 20, she costarred with Val Kilmer in *Batman Forever*. Kilmer's then-wife, Joanne Whalley, subsequently named

Barrymore in her divorce papers when she filed in 1995. See also: Whalley, Joanne.

Batman Forever

The third installment in the Batman revival series of the '80s and '90s. The previous film, Tim Burton's *Batman Returns*, was critically acclaimed, but because of its dark tone and gross, Danny DeVito-related violence, Warner Bros. feared they were missing out on the all important kiddie cash market. For the threequel, they replaced director Burton with Joel Schumacher, in hopes of a more family-friendly outing. See also: gratuitous shots of Val Kilmer in skintight black rubber. See also: Barrymore, Drew.

Blind Horizon

Kind of like *The Bourne Identity* meets *The Manchurian Candidate* meets . . . a movie where Val Kilmer smokes a lot and gets it on with Amy Smart and Neve Campbell. While wearing a cowboy hat.

Depression

The defining characteristic of all mood disorders. "Low" emotion, characterized by lack of energy and motivation, and the inability to feel pleasure.

DSM-IV

The *Diagnostic and Statistical Manual of Mental Disorders*, 4th edition. The American psychology bible, which details the guidelines for diagnosing all mental illnesses.

Heat

A 1995 film from Michael Mann about the leader of a heist crew and the cop pursuing him. Val Kilmer plays a mechanic on the heist crew, and at one point wields a hydraulic saw. You know, if you're into that kind of thing.

Hypomania

The kind of mania experienced by bipolar II patients; the romantic mania of film.

Insomnia

The inability to sleep.

The Island of Dr. Moreau

A 1996 film starring Val Kilmer, Marlon Brando, and David Thewlis, one of many film interpretations of H.G. Wells' book of the same name. Kilmer was originally hired to play the lead role, but was informed of his impending divorce the day after he left for location, and requested a smaller part so he'd have more time to deal with his personal crises. This was only one of many problems Kilmer had onset; director John Frankenheimer did not get along with the actor, and yelled, after calling cut on Kilmer's last scene: "Now get that bastard off my set!"

Kill Me Again

A little noir piece starring Val Kilmer and his then wife, Joanne Whalley. Kilmer plays a down-on-his-luck private eye, and Whalley is the femme fatale who saunters into his office to complicate his life.

Kilmer, Jack

Son of Val Kilmer and Joanne Whalley, born June 6, 1995.

Kilmer, Mercedes

Daughter of Val Kilmer and Joanne Whalley, born October 29, 1991.

Kilmer, Val

An American actor, born December 31, 1959.

Kilmerfest

My own personal Val Kilmer film festival, which took place from September 2010 to March 2011.

Kiss Kiss Bang Bang

A detective caper by Shane Black, starring Val Kilmer and Robert Downey Jr. Kilmer plays a detective called "Gay Perry," three guesses as to why.

Mania

The "high" period of bipolar disorder, characterized by increases of all kinds—more energy, more fun, more arrests.

Mixed State

A feature of bipolar disorder in which both mania and depression are present.

Mood Stabilizer

What your doctor will call an antipsychotic.

Pdoc

Short for "psychiatric doctor," this is crazy people slang for psychiatrist.

Psychiatrist

The doctor who writes your prescriptions. See also: pdoc.

Red Planet

A 2000 science fiction flop about a group of astronauts sent to see if Mars is habitable for humans yet, since they burned out Earth. Kilmer plays a "space janitor" who in reality appears to be about sixteen kinds of engineer and the most helpful person on any planet.

Saint, The

A 1997 film by Philip Noyce. Kilmer plays the eponymous saint, Simon Templar, who is a cat burglar, costume fancier, and wooer of women. Costarring Elisabeth Shue as the most miscast scientist since Denise Richards as a nuclear physicist.

Salton Sea, The

A depressed area of California known for its drug trade. Also a film about said drug trade starring Kilmer as a man trying to avenge his murdered wife.

SI

Short for "self-injury," SI is the purposeful injury of the self, usually by cutting, beating, or burning.

Spartan

A David Mamet picture about a special ops guy fucked over by his country. Kilmer plays Scott, an Army Ranger who will do anything to bring Veronica Mars home.

Suicidal Ideation

Thoughts of suicide.

Therapist

The person you or the state pays to listen to your problems, but cannot write your meds for you.

Therapy

The "talking cure" popularized by Sigmund Freud. A nice alternative to frontal lobe lobotomies, but about as comfortable.

Thunderheart

My favorite Val Kilmer movie, based on the trouble between the FBI and the American Indian Movement in the 1970s. Kilmer plays an FBI agent sent to solve a murder on a reservation because he has Indian blood. There are complications.

Tombstone

A Western women actually like, probably because of Kilmer's Doc Holliday's quick wit and devastating waistline.

Top Gun

A 1986 Tom Cruise vehicle in which Cruise battles daddy issues while grinning maniacally. One of three films Kilmer made with director Tony Scott (the others are *True Romance* and *Déjà vu*.)

Whalley, Joanne

English actress and the former Mrs. Val Kilmer. Joanne Whalley met Kilmer while filming *Willow*, where they were paired as the romantic leads. They married in 1988 and had two children. The couple divorced in 1996, but have since worked together in *Played* (2006) and *Twixt* (2011). See also: Kilmer, Jack; Kilmer, Mercedes.

Willow

A fantasy film by Ron Howard and George Lucas. Kilmer stars as the manic, distractible, constantly-in-trouble Madmartigan, who also happens to be the world's greatest swordsman. Also the meeting place of Kilmer and Joanne Whalley, the English actress he would marry soon after filming completed. See also: Whalley, Joanne.

Lynn Schneider is a published, award-winning author. She earned a bachelor's degree from the University of Tennessee, Knoxville, and an MFA in writing from the Savannah College of Art and Design. She is a dog-enthusiast and natural blonde. She can be reached at c.lynn.schneider@gmail.com.

Made in the USA
Middletown, DE
17 May 2023

30709960R00059